W9-ANQ-566

A Pull Ahead Book

# presidential
# losers

*1470*

David J. Goldman

744138

Steele High School Library
Amherst, Ohio 44001

1470

Lerner Publications Company • Minneapolis, Minnesota

ACKNOWLEDGMENTS: The illustrations are reproduced through the courtesy of: pp. 3, 24, Virginia State Library; pp. 4, 6, 17, 23, 30, 32, 33, 34-35, 40, 41, 42, 43 (bottom), 44, 52, 53, 55, 56, 61, 63, 67, 92, Library of Congress; pp. 5, 46, 73, 74, 75, 82, Independent Picture Service; p. 9, U.S. Capitol Historical Society, pp. 11, 19, 20, New York Public Library; p. 12, New Jersey Historical Society; pp. 15, 21, 29, 38, *Dictionary of American Portraits,* Dover Publications, Inc.; p. 26, The Corcoran Gallery of Art; p. 28, The Metropolitan Museum of Art, Gift of I. N. Phelps Stokes, Edward S. Hawes, Alice Mary Hawes, Marion Augusta Hawes, 1937; p. 36, *Newark News;* p. 43 (top), U.S. Signal Corps, National Archives; p. 48, Culver Pictures, Inc.; pp. 49, 65, Professional Picture Service; p. 51, Rutherford B. Hayes Library; p. 58, Chicago Historical Society; p. 68, Tennessee State Library and Archives; pp. 69, 84, 94, 97, 98, United Press International, Inc.; p. 70, Kansas State Historical Society; p. 72, Ewing Galloway; p. 77, Kansas State University; p. 78, New York Historical Society; pp. 80, 86-87, 96, Wide World Photos; p. 89, Pictorial Parade, Inc.; p. 90, Illinois State Historical Library; pp. 99, 100, United Nations.

The Library of Congress cataloged the
original printing of this title as follows:

Goldman, David J.
  Presidential losers [by] David J. Goldman. Minneapolis, Lerner Publications Co. [1970]

  104 p. illus., ports. 22 cm. (A Pull Ahead Book)

  Brief biographies of eight Presidential candidates who lost the election: Burr, Clay, McClellan, Tilden, Bryan, Landon, Dewey, and Stevenson.

  1. Presidents—U.S.—Election—Juvenile literature. 2. U.S. —Biography—Juvenile literature. [1. Presidents—Election. 2. U.S.—Biography] I. Title.

E183.G6 1970             973 [920]                75-103678
ISBN 0-8225-0457-X                                  MARC

                                                      AC

Copyright © 1970 by Lerner Publications Company. All rights reserved. International copyright secured. Manufactured in the United States of America. Published simultaneously in Canada by J. M. Dent & Sons Ltd., Don Mills, Ontario.

International Standard Book Number: 0-8225-0457-X
Library of Congress Catalog Card Number: 75-103678

Third Printing 1974

# contents

Preface . . . . . . . . . . . . . . . .   5

Who Elects the
   President? . . . . . . . . . . .   7

Aaron Burr . . . . . . . . . . . . .  13

Henry Clay . . . . . . . . . . . . .  25

George B. McClellan . . . . .  37

Samuel Tilden . . . . . . . . . .  47

William Jennings Bryan . . .  59

Alfred M. Landon . . . . . . . .  71

Thomas E. Dewey . . . . . . .  79

Adlai Stevenson . . . . . . . .  91

Some Facts About the
   Electoral College . . . . . .101

Henry Clay

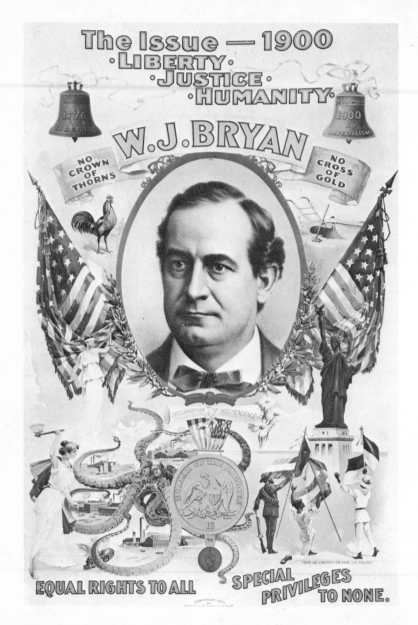

A campaign poster for William Jennings Bryan. The election of 1900 was the second of Bryan's three unsuccessful tries for the presidency.

Wendell L. Willkie

Alfred E. Smith

# preface

A political comeback is extremely rare in United States presidential history. Richard Nixon was the first man since William Henry Harrison to win the presidency after losing a previous election. Only two other men, Andrew Jackson and Thomas Jefferson, have been elected President after being defeated. Usually a presidential loser never gets any closer to the presidency than he was on election day.

The first presidential losers I selected for this book were those who ran at least twice without success (Henry Clay, William Jennings Bryan, Thomas E. Dewey, and Adlai Stevenson). I then chose a loser who should have won (Samuel Tilden) as an example of the irony, complexity, and occasional unfairness of the electoral process. Two men who ran at particularly meaningful times in the nation's history were also selected (George B. McClellan and Alfred M. Landon). Finally, I included a loser whose story I found especially interesting (Aaron Burr).

Other losers also have interesting stories. Horace Greeley was nominated by the party he hated. Charles Evans Hughes went to bed certain that he had won, but he awoke to learn that the returns from California and Minnesota had put Woodrow Wilson in the White House instead. To a majority of voters, Alfred E. Smith's more obvious characteristics — he was a Catholic, a "wet," and a product of the city—overshadowed his efficiency and intelligence. Wendell L. Willkie, a former Democrat and a dark horse, was unable to keep Franklin D. Roosevelt from a third term. Unfortunately, it was impossible to include all of the men who came so close to the nation's highest office.

DAVID J. GOLDMAN
*Washington, D.C.*

For several years, only men who were wealthy or who owned land could vote for President of the United States. By 1828, the year Andrew Jackson was elected President, many states allowed every white male to vote. This drawing shows Andrew Jackson, the newly elected President, greeting the people on his way to Washington, D.C.

## Who Elects the President?

We say "the majority rules" in the United States. The candidate most of the people vote for, even if he is Alfred E. Neuman or Pat Paulsen, wins the presidency. But this is not always true. Someday you might vote for a man (or perhaps a woman) who gets most of the votes from the people but does not become President. This has happened in the United States three times. The last time was in 1888, but it could happen in any presidential election.

How can the man who gets the most votes not be President? The answer to this question lies in the complicated way that the United States chooses its President. The American people do not really elect the President. The Electoral College does.

The Electoral College is not a school, but a group of men and women who never meet together. All they do is vote for the President every four years. When you vote for a presidential candidate, you are really just choosing a set of electors. If you vote for the Republican candidate, you are saying, "I want the electors from the Republican party, not the Democratic party, or any other party, to be in the Electoral College from my state." If the Republican candidate wins a majority of the votes in your state, the Republican set of electors votes for President. Electors mail their votes to Washington, D.C., where the President of the United States Senate counts them. The electoral college system is discussed further on page 101.

The United States Senate in session. In January after each presidential election, the President of the Senate counts the votes of the Electoral College. The Senators and the Representatives meet in the House chamber to witness the counting of the votes.

Someday you might vote for a man who gets the majority of votes in your state, but the electors from your state do not vote for him in the Electoral College. This can happen because in many states the electors can vote for any man they want to, whether he wins in their state or not. Fortunately, the electors usually vote the way the majority voted.

Many people would like to get rid of the Electoral College and have the people choose the President directly. This probably will happen in your lifetime. When it does, elections will be less complicated. But they may be less interesting. As this book will show, having the Electoral College choose the President sometimes leads to unexpected results.

George Washington, first President of the United States. He was elected for two terms, and both times all the members of the Electoral College voted for him.

Since the birth of the nation, there have been 46 presidential elections. No one ran against George Washington, the first President. But in every election after the first two, someone tried for the presidency and was defeated. Some of the losers were later elected President. Some became famous even though they never were President. Others were never heard from again. Whatever happened to them in later years, these men all shared a common bond. They had the privilege of running for the nation's highest office. That is honor enough for most men.

## Aaron Burr
(1756-1836)

Aaron Burr is the most unusual of all the presidential losers. He tried to trick his party into electing him President — and he almost succeeded. All his life Burr was a power-hungry man. He did not care *how* he got power, just so he got it. This led him to do things that were not completely honest.

Burr was a leading member of the Anti-Federalist party in New York State. This party, led by Thomas Jefferson, was formed to oppose the Federalists, who were led by Alexander Hamilton. (These were the first political parties in the United States.) The Federalists thought that only the rich and well-educated people were good enough to run the government. They wanted the government in Washington to be very powerful. The Anti-Federalists believed that the common people should have a say in the government. They also wanted the states to have as much power as the federal government.

Burr got his chance for the presidency in the election of 1800. The Anti-Federalists decided that Jefferson should run for President and Burr for Vice President. Jefferson was from Virginia, so he would get votes from the South. Burr was from New York, so the North would support him.

Burr agreed to run for Vice President, but he knew that it was an office without much influence or power. He began to make secret plans to get himself elected President instead of Jefferson.

What Burr tried to do is impossible today because the rules for electing a President have been changed. Until 1804 every candidate for President or Vice President ran by himself. There were no "tickets." Each elector voted for two men separately. The man who got the most votes was President, and the man who came in second was Vice President. If there was a tie, the House of Representatives chose the President. Burr decided that he would try to make the election a tie in the Electoral College. He had as many friends in the House as Jefferson did, and he thought he could win the presidency there.

Thomas Jefferson, third President of the United States. He was almost Vice President instead.

The Anti-Federalists asked Burr to make sure that one or two of the Anti-Federalist electors voted for Jefferson but not for Burr. That would put Jefferson in as President with Burr as Vice President. Burr told his party members that he would take care of it. But he did not. When the results came in, they were just what Burr had hoped for. All the electors who voted for Jefferson also voted for Burr. The vote in the Electoral College was tied 73 to 73. Burr, who was supposed to be Vice President, was now almost President.

The House of Representatives was asked to choose between Jefferson and Burr. In 1800 there were more Federalists in the House than Anti-Federalists. Although the Federalists themselves had lost the election, they had to decide who would be the next President. Burr probably could have stepped aside and let Jefferson be the President. After all, he had been nominated only for Vice President. But Burr refused to do so.

This was the first election in the nation's history in which the House of Representatives had to decide the winner. The Constitution says that when an election goes to the House, each state gets one vote. The Representatives from each state get together in a group and vote. The candidate who wins in that group gets the one vote from that state. In the election of 1800, there were only 16 states. The candidate who received nine votes would win.

When the House met to choose the President, Jefferson got eight votes on the first ballot, and Burr got six. Two states, Vermont and Maryland, did not vote for either man. The Representatives from these states were split evenly, half for Jefferson, and half for Burr. Jefferson needed one more vote to win; Burr needed three. Over a period of a week, the House voted 35 times, and each time the results were the same — eight for Jefferson, six for Burr, and two undecided.

Alexander Hamilton, leader of the Federalist party. He helped Jefferson to be elected instead of Burr. Four years later Burr killed Hamilton in a duel.

The Federalists realized that they had to come to a decision. Hamilton, as the Federalist leader, had to choose between his two enemies, Jefferson and Burr. He hated Jefferson and his party, but he was afraid of Aaron Burr. He knew that Burr was a dishonest man who was more interested in having power than in serving his country. Hamilton was also jealous of Burr's power in his home state of New York. So he got his friends in the House to vote for Jefferson. On the 36th ballot, the votes from Vermont and Maryland went to Jefferson. Jefferson was elected President, and Burr became Vice President.

While the voting was going on, Burr kept silent. If he had promised to work for the Federalist ideas, he might have swung the vote to his side. Instead, he did nothing, realizing that he would be finished with the Anti-Federalists if he made any kind of deal. Burr accepted the office of Vice President, but he never forgave Alexander Hamilton for helping Jefferson to become President.

In the next four years, Burr served as a fair and dignified Vice President. But he had made many political enemies. President Jefferson was unfriendly to him, because he was sure that Burr had tried to trick him. Also, Burr and Hamilton began to hate each other. They called each other names in public, in letters, and in the newspapers. Their attacks became more and more vicious. Hamilton called Burr "a dangerous man" and accused him of planning to overthrow the government. In 1804, his last year as Vice President, Burr ran for governor of New York. The bad feelings between Hamilton and Burr became even worse when Burr lost the election to the man Hamilton supported.

Burr and Hamilton face each other in their duel. It is possible that Hamilton deliberately aimed the pistol away from Burr. However, Burr took direct aim and did not miss.

Finally Burr became uncontrollably angry. He challenged Hamilton to a duel in July 1804. The two men met early one morning in an empty field near Weehawken, New Jersey. Pistols were chosen as the weapons. Burr and Hamilton walked away from each other, turned, and fired. Burr proved to be the better shot, and he badly wounded Hamilton. The next day Hamilton died.

Hamilton and Burr used these pistols in their duel.

The country was shocked. The Vice President had killed one of the nation's first great leaders. Burr finished his term of office, but he was no longer a popular man. Realizing that he could never be President, he began to look for another way to gain power. He traveled in the southern and southwestern parts of the country and started making some mysterious plans. Historians believe that Burr may have planned to capture Mexico and make a kingdom for himself. Or he may have plotted a rebellion of the western states against the East. A third possibility is that Burr hoped to take over some land between Louisiana and Mexico.

James Wilkinson, Burr's partner in a secret plan. Wilkinson later told President Jefferson about the plan, and Burr was arrested.

In the summer of 1806 Burr and 60 men began a trip down the Ohio and Mississippi rivers in 13 flatboats. But Burr never was able to carry out his plans, whatever they were. One of his co-plotters, General James Wilkinson, betrayed Burr in order to make some money. He sent a letter to President Jefferson, telling him that Burr was going to attack New Orleans on his way to Mexico. Burr tried to run away but was caught in South Carolina. The President had Burr arrested and charged with treason.

Burr went on trial in Richmond, Virginia, in March 1807. The trial caused a great stir of excitement. Chief Justice John Marshall was the judge. Burr was found not guilty and set free because there was no evidence that he had done anything against the government. Most Americans, however, still believed that Burr was a traitor. After the trial Burr went to France and tried to get Napoleon to help him capture some land in America. When this failed, Burr went back to New York and started practicing law again. He lived in New York for nearly 20 years more, but never returned to public life.

Aaron Burr had this portrait painted when he was 78 years old.

H. Clay

# Henry Clay

(1777-1852)

Henry Clay's career in public life lasted nearly 50 years. During that time he did everything he could to become President, but he never succeeded. He ran for the presidency and was defeated in 1824, 1832, and 1844. Clay was the first three-time presidential loser. Only one other man, William Jennings Bryan, ran and lost three times.

Henry Clay was an ambitious young man. He began to practice law when he was 20 years old, and when he was 26 he was elected to the Kentucky state legislature. Next he ran for the United States House of Representatives. The Kentucky voters liked him, and he was easily elected. He served his state well in Congress.

Clay had a powerful personality. He was a ladies' man, a storyteller, a poker player, and a big drinker. He quickly became one of the most important men in Washington. In 1811, after Clay had been in Washington less than five years, the House of Representatives elected him to be their Speaker. (The Speaker takes charge of running the meetings of the House.)

A painting of the House of Representatives in 1822. Clay, as Speaker, sat on the platform at the left. The House soon grew too large for this chamber, which today is used to display statues of famous Americans.

In 1816 Clay used his power to help James Monroe win the presidency. For his efforts, Clay hoped to be named Secretary of State. He was sure that if he could be Secretary of State, he would then be elected President. All four Presidents after George Washington had first been Secretary of State. But Monroe gave the job to John Quincy Adams. Clay was very disappointed. He became hard to work with and used his power to make things difficult for President Monroe. For example, he did not let President Monroe take the oath of office inside the House building. And he refused to attend the ceremony. Clay never forgave people who crossed him.

Clay ran for the presidency for the first time in 1824, but he came in last in a four-man race. That year no candidate won a majority of votes in the Electoral College. The leading candidates were Andrew Jackson, who got 99 votes, and John Quincy Adams, who got 84. The third candidate, William Crawford, had 41 votes, and Clay had only 37.

John Quincy Adams, sixth President of the
United States. Many people believed that
Adams made a deal with Clay to get himself
elected. This photograph was taken in 1848.
*(Courtesy The Metropolitan Museum of Art)*

Even though Clay got the least number of votes, he
came close to winning the presidency. The Constitution says
that when no candidate wins an election the House of Representatives must vote on the three candidates with the most
votes. If Clay had received four more electoral votes, he
would have come in third. Then he would have been considered for the presidency along with Jackson and Adams.
And he could have won in the House because he was so
popular there.

William Crawford came in third in the four-man race for President in 1824.

Clay's popularity in the House did mean that he had the power to decide which man would be President in 1824. Clay did not consider Crawford, because he had a serious illness. Andrew Jackson had received the largest number of popular votes, and thus he really deserved to be President. But Clay did not want him to win. Jackson was from the West, like Clay. Clay hoped to end Jackson's political career in 1824, so that Clay would have the full support of the West the next time he ran for President. However, Clay did not really like Adams either. He had not forgotten that Monroe had chosen Adams to be Secretary of State instead of Clay. But Clay finally decided to throw his strength to Adams, who was thus elected.

Andrew Jackson, seventh President of the United States. He did not become President in 1824 but won the next two presidential elections.

President Adams, in turn, made Clay his Secretary of State. Many people, especially Jackson and his supporters, became angry with Clay. It looked as if he had made a deal with Adams. Clay served as Secretary of State for four years, but the job did not please him. He retired from public life when Jackson became President in 1829. But Prince Harry, as Clay was sometimes called, still hoped to be President. He did not stay out of politics for long. Clay went back to Washington as a Senator in 1831.

The next year Clay was chosen by the Whigs, a new political party, to run for President. Both the Whigs and the Democrats held nominating conventions in 1832. This was the first time that members of each party met together to choose the men they wanted to have run for President and Vice President. The Democrats chose Andrew Jackson to run for a second term. Clay was a charming and powerful candidate, but the people loved Jackson, and he easily won the election. Jackson received 219 votes in the Electoral College; Clay had only 49.

After his second presidential defeat Clay returned to the Senate, where he was still highly respected. But in spite of his popularity and power, Clay became increasingly bitter. He was angry about his two defeats for the presidency. He wanted to run again in 1840. But the Whigs decided that Clay could not win, and they chose another man, William Henry Harrison. Clay was asked to be the vice presidential candidate, but he refused. Harrison won the election and died one month after taking office. This was the first of two times that Clay turned down the nomination for Vice President. Both times the Whigs won the election. Both times the man who was elected President died in office, and Clay would have become President.

Henry Clay's election banner for the 1844 Whig party convention. The 1844 election was Clay's third try for the presidency.

James Poik, 11th President of the United States. He was the first presidential "dark horse."

Clay did not give up his desire for the presidency, even though his party had not nominated him in 1840. He still had great power in the Whig party, and he gained the nomination for himself in 1844. By this time he was 67 years old, but he ran for the office with energy. Once again he was defeated. This time he lost to James Polk, the first presidential "dark horse." Polk was called a dark horse because he was not nationally known and had not been considered for the nomination until his party's convention had already started.

Henry Clay speaks to the United States Senate in 1850. Because of his efforts to keep the North and the South together, Clay was named the Great Compromiser.

Clay's spirit seemed to fade after his third defeat. But he was too much a fighter to stay away from politics. He returned to the Senate in 1849 and stayed there until he died in 1852.

Clay is remembered as the Great Pacificator or Great Compromiser. After the 1820s the United States began to be divided, the North against the South, over the problem of slavery. Three times between 1820 and 1850 Clay worked

out plans to help the North and the South settle their differences without war. Partly because of Clay's work, the Civil War was not fought in his lifetime.

Clay served his country for many years, but never as its President. Few men in history, however, have held as much power in the Senate as Clay did. In 1957 the United States Senate voted Clay one of the five greatest Senators in the country's history.

# George B. McClellan
(1826-1885)

Many generals have run for the presidency. George Washington, Andrew Jackson, and Dwight D. Eisenhower were generals who later became Presidents. They had become famous and respected by helping the United States win in war. Other well-known generals ran for President and lost. General George B. McClellan was one of the losers. But his story is unusual. He was not a good general; he had been fired from his job two years before the presidential election.

When the Civil War broke out, McClellan was made a major general in the Northern army and was given command of the Ohio area. At first he was a successful military leader, perhaps because he did not have to fight against very large armies. He drove the Southern forces out of Ohio and western Virginia. McClellan was the only Northern general who won any battles in 1861, the first year of the Civil War.

Abraham Lincoln, 16th President of the United States. Lincoln said of McClellan, "He has got the slows."

McClellan's victories on the western front brought him to the attention of President Lincoln. In August 1861 Lincoln gave McClellan command of the Army of the Potomac, the Union forces in the East. McClellan's job was to organize this part of the Northern army. The soldiers of this army had been badly defeated in their first battle. They were discouraged, and most of them were not trained for fighting. McClellan took them and created one of the finest armies in the world. He organized and trained it perfectly, and he got only the best equipment for his men. His soldiers trusted and respected their leader. McClellan loved to parade his troops through the streets of Washington.

Steele High School Library
Amherst, Ohio 44001

In November 1861 Lincoln appointed McClellan commander over all the sections of the Northern army. McClellan believed that he had been called to save the Union from destruction. He was convinced that he was a great soldier and the only man who was able to win the war for the North. He read everything he could about Napoleon, and sometimes he believed that he was like the French Emperor. Both men were short and stocky. The newspapers often called McClellan the Young Napoleon. McClellan thought that his early victories in Ohio and western Virginia proved what a good general he really was. Just as Napoleon had saved France, McClellan would save the Union.

It was true that McClellan was very good at organizing and training soldiers. But he had one weakness as a general. He would almost never fight. He was too cautious and fearful to attack the Southern army. And the Young Napoleon could not be made to lead his men into battle when they did fight. Many times he was far behind the lines when the firing began. Once, he slept right through a battle.

McClellan was also a difficult man to work with. He argued constantly with the other generals. Lincoln could not make him listen to his orders and advice. Finally, in March 1862, Lincoln removed McClellan from command of the Union forces, leaving him in charge of only the Army of the Potomac.

Union soldiers charge at the Battle of Antietam.

McClellan became very discouraged in his new position; he was afraid that he would not be able to win the war. But he received a second chance to try. After the Union forces were badly defeated once more, the President asked McClellan to become commander of the entire army again. The Union forces in both the East and the West were not doing well. Lincoln chose McClellan because none of the other Northern generals were any more successful than he was.

Dead soldiers after the Battle of Antietam

McClellan's performance as a general was better the second time. The Southern forces, under General Robert E. Lee, were moving into the North. Even the city of Washington was in danger. In September 1862 McClellan stopped the invasion of Lee's army at Antietam in Maryland. The Young Napoleon finally won a victory. However, if a better general had been in McClellan's place, the Civil War might have been over at the Battle of Antietam. Unfortunately, the Civil War lasted for two and one half more years.

President Lincoln talks with McClellan on the battlefield at Antietam.

Military experts say that McClellan should have attacked Lee's soldiers as they retreated. But McClellan grew timid again. He was satisfied when he saw the Southern army leave.

President Lincoln still was not happy with McClellan. He wanted to win the war, not just to have the city of Washington defended. Lincoln asked McClellan to move south to fight the Confederates. McClellan put off starting for a whole month. Once again, in November 1862, Lincoln dismissed McClellan, this time forever. The President said, "He has got the slows."

Above: General Ulysses S. Grant (left) and other Union officers. President Lincoln said of Grant, "He fights."

Below: General Robert E. Lee (fourth from right) and his Confederate officers. Lee was one of the most brilliant military leaders in United States history. Seated is Jefferson Davis, President of the Confederacy.

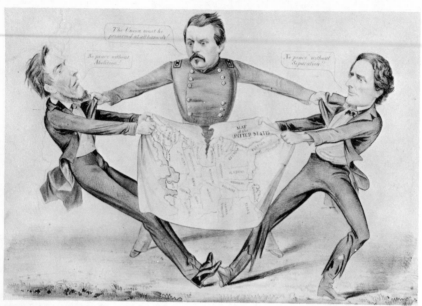

A cartoon from the election of 1864. McClellan, in the center, tries to keep President Lincoln and the President of the Confederacy, Jefferson Davis, from tearing the country apart.

McClellan became upset with the Union and President Lincoln. He thought that he was a good general. Besides, he had not wanted Lincoln to free the slaves. He had always liked the more formal Southern ways. But McClellan did want to save the Union and bring back the Southern states. He would do it all alone, if necessary. His desire for power was growing. If he could not save the nation as a general, he would save it by becoming President.

McClellan began to attack President Lincoln. He called him "a well-meaning baboon," and "the original gorilla."

The Democrats decided that the 38-year-old general would be a good candidate to run against Lincoln for the presidency in 1864. The people were tired of the war. President Lincoln was becoming less popular. The general was nominated by the Democrats at their convention in Chicago. McClellan was popular with many voters. Even Lincoln said that he did not see how McClellan could be beaten.

Luckily for Lincoln, the war took a turn in the Union's favor. Generals Sheridan, Sherman, and Grant began to win the battles that McClellan had been too cautious to start. The South was in retreat by the time the election was held. President Lincoln was re-elected, but he did not receive a large majority. The vote showed that many people agreed with McClellan. They believed that the little general with the mustache was the right man to save the Union, even though he had not been a successful general.

After his defeat, McClellan returned to private life. He spent several years traveling in Europe and then became chief engineer for the New York City docks. From 1878 to 1881 he served as governor of New Jersey. Throughout his life he had many business interests which were very successful. One of his projects was designing a subway system for New York City, but his plan was never used. During his last years he wrote a book about his part in the Civil War. McClellan died in 1884. He was never able to convince the nation of the greatness he was sure he possessed.

S. J. Tilden

## Samuel Tilden

(1814-1886)

Samuel Tilden was elected President, but he never took office and never served. He lived in a time of great dishonesty and corruption in local, state, and national government. He was cheated out of the presidency by a political deal.

Tilden became famous by fighting against corruption in the city and state governments of New York. In the early 1870s New York was run by a man called Boss Tweed. He held great power in the city and the state, and he used it to make himself and his friends rich. Tweed and his men "padded" payrolls by adding people who did not exist and collecting their wages. They received "kickbacks" from contracts; part of the tax money paid to a contractor would go into the pocket of the man who set up the contract. Elections were "fixed." Tweed paid people to vote the "right" way, and often his men used force to get votes. Sometimes election officials reported the results without even counting the ballots. Once Tweed put his governor of New York into office with more votes than there were voters. Even the judges in New York did what Boss Tweed told them to. Honest New Yorkers did not see any way to get rid of the Tweed "machine."

Boss Tweed. The Tweed Ring cheated New Yorkers of at least 30 million dollars.

Tilden and his followers began to work for reform and improvement of city and state politics. They started with the Tweed Ring. Their first move was to get honest men elected judges. Then they took Boss Tweed and his ring to court and published their crimes in newspapers. Tweed was sent to jail. The thankful citizens elected Tilden governor of New York in 1874. Then he attacked another group of political crooks, the Canal Ring. These men ran the Erie Canal and were also cheating the taxpayers. Tilden took care of this ring as quickly as he did the Tweed Ring.

A cartoon showing Boss Tweed and his ring as vultures. They are standing on the body of New York. The dead skulls and bones of justice, liberty, law, the taxpayer, and the rent-payer lie on the ground in front of them. The cartoon is entitled "Let Us Prey."

Political campaigns of the 1870s involved heavy gambling. On this poster a man named George Marlette announces that he is betting Rutherford B. Hayes will beat Samuel J. Tilden. Marlette collected.

The federal government, under President Ulysses S. Grant, was also corrupt during the 1870s. Dishonest politicians and businessmen were stealing millions of dollars from the federal treasury. Two of Grant's closest advisors were involved in the theft, and they were not even punished. Tilden, the great reformer, looked like the man to clean up Washington. The Democrats nominated him for the presidency in 1876. The Republican candidate was Rutherford B. Hayes.

Both parties ran dirty campaigns, as was natural in the politics of that time. The Democrats talked about the dishonesty of Grant's Republican government, although things were probably not as bad as they said. The Republicans "waved the bloody shirt." They reminded people of the terrible events of the Civil War, and they said that the Democrats had sided with the "rebels" and therefore were not loyal Americans. Many Republicans whispered that Tilden was "a drunkard, a liar, a cheat, a counterfeiter."

When the votes were counted on election day, Tilden looked like the winner. Newspapers all over the country reported that he was the 19th President. Tilden had beaten Hayes by a quarter of a million popular votes. But in electoral votes, Tilden had 184 and Hayes had 166. To win the election, one candidate needed 185 electoral votes. Nineteen electoral votes were still in doubt. In South Carolina, Louisiana, and Florida both the Democrats and the Republicans claimed victory.

An election banner for Samuel J. Tilden

Tilden needed only one more electoral vote to win. If Hayes received all the votes from the three states, he would win. The stalemate started the greatest political "wheeling and dealing" of the century. Money was sent from the North to help the electors make the right decision. Bribes

LIBERTY AND UNION

GOV. RUTHERFORD B. HAYES.

HON. WM. A. WHEELER.

FOR PRESIDENT.

FOR VICE-PRESIDENT.

Copyright 1876, by Currier & Ives, N.Y.

GRAND NATIONAL REPUBLICAN BANNER.

An election banner for Rutherford B. Hayes

and promises of good federal jobs were made to the local officials. Finally, on December 6, Republican electors met in the three states and voted for Hayes. But on the same day three sets of Democratic electors met and cast votes for Tilden.

The celebration in Washington, D.C., after Hayes was sworn in as President. Not all of the voters were happy, however.

The whole problem was sent to Congress for a decision. The Constitution does not say what to do when states cannot decide who has received the most votes. So a special commission was selected to decide who had really won the election. Fifteen men were chosen for the commission — five Representatives, five Senators, and five Supreme Court Justices. The commission was supposed to be split evenly between the two parties — seven Republicans and seven Democrats. The 15th man, a judge, was supposed to be neutral, neither a Republican nor a Democrat. Just before the commission met, the neutral judge was elected to a Senate seat. Since he was a Senator, he was ruled out of the commission. The empty place was taken by a Republican, giving Hayes's supporters a one-vote advantage.

The commission decided, by a vote of eight to seven, that Hayes had won in South Carolina, Louisiana, and Florida. All 19 electoral votes went to Hayes, who then had 185 votes to Tilden's 184. Hayes was the new President by one electoral vote.

Rutherford B. Hayes, 19th President of the United States. He became President even though more people had voted for Tilden.

The Democrats were furious. At first they refused to accept the decision. But behind the scenes, a deal was made. The Southern Democrats were shown that it would be good for their party if the Republican candidate became President. They were promised many special favors. One favor was the removal of all the Union troops that had been stationed in the South since the Civil War. This meant that the Republicans would no longer be in control of the Southern state governments. The Southern Democrats decided not to oppose Hayes. They accepted the deal offered by the Hayes supporters. The Northern Democrats were thus forced to give in also. Hayes was officially declared President just two days before he was sworn in.

The nation was shocked. The people clearly wanted Tilden; he had received a majority of the popular vote. The politicians, not the people, had decided that Hayes would be President. Tilden's party workers screamed "Robbery!" They staged many parades and rallies. But Tilden refused even to make a comment. He remained silent and watched from a distance. Tilden feared that another civil war would break out if the election became too big an issue. Also, Tilden knew that many of the Democrats were no more honest than the Republicans. In the South, they had kept many Negroes away from the polls on election day to prevent them from voting for the Republican candidate.

Tilden accepted the politicians' decision calmly, and he returned to private life. Since his supporters had no leader, the excitement passed away. More than any of the presidential losers, Samuel Tilden deserved to be President —he actually had been elected. But the game of politics is not always fair.

(Courtesy Chicago Historical Society)

W.J. Bryan

# William Jennings Bryan
(1860-1925)

Probably the most famous of all presidential losers is William Jennings Bryan. He is the only other three-time loser besides Henry Clay, and the first one from the Democratic party. Bryan ran for the presidency in 1896, 1900, and 1908. He was popular because he seemed very much like an average American. In fact, many people called him the Great Commoner. But Bryan was unusual in one important way; he was the greatest public speaker of his time.

Bryan's favorite cause was "free silver" coinage. He wanted the government to use more silver for money. In 1873 the United States had gone on the gold standard. Gold, not silver, was used to back up paper money and make dollar coins. This meant that the amount of money available to the people was limited by the amount of gold the United States Treasury could get. In 1878 the Treasury began buying some silver and using it for dollars, but the amount of silver it could buy was limited by law. Thus there still was not much money available in the 1880s and 1890s. Bryan believed that free silver coinage, with no limit to the amount of silver the Treasury could buy, would bring more money to the common people.

A campaign poster for William Jennings Bryan. Below Bryan's wife and children is a copy of his "cross of gold" speech.

The Americans who were poorest at this time were the Midwestern and Southern farmers. These were the common people that Bryan was closest to. He believed that if the government kept the gold standard the farmers and workers would get even poorer. But having free silver coinage would bring them more money and a better living.

In 1894 Bryan ran for the United States Senate and lost. But he was not finished in politics. His greatest moment was yet to come. In 1896 the Democratic party held its national convention in Chicago. As in every convention, the delegates had to decide what causes they were going to support. The Midwesterners were free silver men, but the Democrats from the East supported the gold standard. The delegates could agree on hardly anything. Bryan was scheduled to talk on the free silver question. He was the last of six speakers. His moment had arrived. He filled the hall with his mighty voice, telling the delegates about the evil of the gold standard. The delegates at first sat still, as if he had cast a spell on them. Then they grew wild with excitement, roaring with approval. They cheered and yelled at every line. "You shall not press down upon the brow of labor this crown of thorns, you shall not crucify mankind upon a cross of gold!" he concluded.

The delegates accepted free silver, and they also found a new leader. Bryan was nominated for the presidency on the fifth ballot. He had barely been able to get a seat in the convention hall. But with one overpowering speech, he became the Democratic candidate.

Bryan's success was really not so surprising. He was a skillful speaker, but this speech was not new. In fact, Bryan had given parts of it before. He had been making speeches in the West and the South for three years, to get people interested in the free silver cause. Bryan knew that he could capture the delegates if he had a chance to speak. His "cross of gold" speech is one of the most famous political speeches ever given in America.

After Bryan accepted the nomination at the convention, he started a blazing campaign. He was one of the first presidential candidates to visit many parts of the country. He traveled more than 18,000 miles and gave as many as 31 speeches a day. Over 5 million people heard him speak in person. His tall, broad-shouldered frame and his large head made him a handsome figure. With his booming voice and powerful speaking style, Bryan swayed the people.

William McKinley was the Republican candidate who ran against Bryan for the presidency. His campaign was managed by a sharp Ohio businessman named Mark Hanna.

William McKinley, 25th President of the United States. He was assassinated during his second term of office.

Hanna got large gifts of money from eastern businessmen who did not want Bryan to be President. He used some of this money to bring groups of people to McKinley's house. McKinley stood on his front porch and spoke to each group. Sometimes the campaign of 1896 became dirty. A favorite Republican chant was:

> *McKinley drinks soda water,*
> *Bryan drinks rum.*
> *McKinley is a gentleman,*
> *Bryan is a bum.*

Although this rhyme was probably not true, Bryan and McKinley were very different from each other.

In this cartoon Bryan, a knight in shining armor, meets defeat when he tries to knock over McKinley's "Full Dinner Pail."

McKinley was a candidate for the businessmen, the rich people, and the Easterners. Bryan represented the farmers, the poor people, and the Midwesterners. Bryan had great fondness for the common people. He cared more for people than he did for issues or ideas. He fought for free silver because he believed that it would make things better for the farmers and the workers. But Bryan could also be prejudiced and narrow-minded. For example, he openly disliked Negroes. He was a man of more emotion than reason.

McKinley won the election by a good margin. Bryan's exciting speeches were not enough. Still, Bryan kept control of the Democratic party. He wanted to run for President in the next election. During the time McKinley was President, Bryan went on speaking tours all over the country. His silver-tongued speeches still brought the people out in great numbers. He continued to support free silver, and he also spoke out against American control of the Philippines after the Spanish-American War (1898-1900). His speeches kept people from forgetting him.

In 1900 Bryan again ran for the presidency. But by that year good times had returned to the country. The farmers and the workers were not as poor as they had been in 1896.

President McKinley took advantage of the plentiful period. He campaigned on the slogan "A Full Dinner Pail," reminding the people that good times had come while he was President. Bryan was defeated again, but he remained an important man in the Democratic party.

William Howard Taft, 27th President of the United States. He was the winner in Bryan's third try for the presidency.

In 1904 Bryan did not seek the nomination for the presidency. The Democratic candidate was Alton B. Parker, a New York judge who did not support the free silver cause. Bryan did very little to help Parker win. He quietly hoped that Theodore Roosevelt, the Republican candidate, would win, so that he could get the Democratic nomination for himself in 1908. His wish came true. Parker did lose the election, and four years later the Democrats nominated Bryan to run again.

Thus, in 1908 Bryan was a presidential candidate for the third time. But he was no longer the sharp, exciting man he had been in 1896. He was not a dashing 36-year-old; he was 48. His face was less handsome, his whole appearance was not attractive, and his speaking ability was starting to fade. His moment had come and gone in 1896. William Howard Taft, although he was no beauty at 332 pounds, easily won the election for the Republicans. William Jennings Bryan never ran for President again.

But Bryan could not stay out of the national spotlight. He used his power in the Democratic party to get the presidential nomination for Woodrow Wilson in 1912. When Wilson was elected, he chose Bryan to be his Secretary of State. Bryan served until he and the President could no

longer agree on what the United States should do about World War I, which was then being fought in Europe. Bryan was completely against war and did not want Wilson to take sides against Germany. In 1915 he resigned.

William Jennings Bryan at the Scopes trial in Tennessee

The last episode in Bryan's life made him more well known, but it also was embarrassing to him. In 1925 Bryan took part in the Scopes trial in Tennessee. John T. Scopes was on trial for teaching the theory of evolution. This theory says that modern plants and animals evolved from earlier ones. Bryan and his followers could not accept the possibility that man came from monkeys or apes. Bryan believed in the account of creation in the Bible, which says that men came from Adam and Eve. He had always been a deeply religious man, but his beliefs were narrow-minded. He could

Clarence Darrow, a famous criminal lawyer who defended Scopes in the "monkey trial." Darrow lost the case, but his cross-examination made Bryan's beliefs seem foolish.

not easily accept the views of others. During the 1920s Bryan had helped to get laws passed in several Southern states forbidding anyone to teach the theory of evolution in school.

When Scopes was brought to trial, Bryan worked to get him convicted. Clarence Darrow, a skillful lawyer, defended Scopes. The whole country became interested in the results of the "monkey trial." Bryan's side won; Scopes was found guilty of breaking the law and fined $100. But it really was a defeat, not a victory, for Bryan. When Darrow cross-examined him, Bryan seemed ignorant and foolish. Bryan knew almost nothing about modern science. He came out of the trial a broken man. Five days later he died.

William Jennings Bryan never became President, but many of the ideas he worked for became laws, including greater use of silver, an income tax, and the vote for women.

# Alfred M. Landon

(1887-     )

Many men have lost presidential elections. Some have lost more than once. Most are forgotten. A few are remembered because of other accomplishments in their lives. One man, Alfred Landon, is remembered just because he had the greatest presidential defeat in United States history.

Landon became a Kansas oil millionaire during the 1920s. This period in American history is known as the Roaring Twenties, because the country became very wealthy and many people were enjoying good times. Then, in 1929, the economy went bad. Banks closed, and businesses became bankrupt. Millions of people were out of work. Many lost their homes, and some nearly starved. This period is called the Great Depression. Conditions became worse from 1929 to 1932, and the Republican President, Herbert Hoover, was unable to solve the nation's problems. In 1932 the American voters elected Franklin D. Roosevelt, a Democrat, to be President. In the same year the voters of Kansas elected Republican Alf Landon to be their governor.

A jobless worker sells an apple for a nickel. During the Great Depression many men sold apples in order to have money to feed their families.

President Roosevelt gave the country what he called a New Deal. He created many new programs and began spending government money in order to bring back good times. But Landon kept things about the same in Kansas. He did not believe that the government should spend large amounts of money to improve economic conditions. He kept the Kansas state government from spending more money than it took in. As governor, Landon always had his door open to the people. He was happy to listen to their problems. The people of Kansas liked Landon; he was a sensible businessman. In 1934 he was the only Republican governor re-elected in the whole country.

Franklin D. Roosevelt, 32nd President of the United States. His warm personality made him popular with many people.

In 1936 President Roosevelt was up for re-election. The people would decide whether they liked the reform programs of the New Deal. The Republicans were hopeful of victory. They nominated the best known man in their party, Alfred Landon.

President Roosevelt arrives in Philadelphia to give his speech accepting the 1936 Democratic nomination for President.

Landon was popular with the Kansas voters because he was able to get out and meet the people. But it was impossible for him to meet nearly 130 million Americans. Both presidential candidates had to reach the people by radio. Landon did not do well on the radio. His voice was dull, slow, and boring. President Roosevelt was the opposite. His voice came over the radio in a warm, friendly manner.

Landon tried to please the nation the same way he had pleased the people of Kansas. He offered himself as a simple

Mr. and Mrs. Alfred Landon at home in Kansas after the Republican convention of 1936 had chosen Landon as the presidential candidate.

small-town businessman, an honest politician who was close to the people. He would balance the nation's budget and save money in government. Two of his campaign slogans were "Save the American Way of Life" and "Life, Liberty, and Landon." But his speeches, like his radio broadcasts, were uninteresting and awkward. President Roosevelt was a much better campaigner. He was clever and quick, and he knew how to use his power and personality. Large crowds cheered him wherever he went.

Some political experts began to predict the election winners before the election was held. They asked a number of people how they were going to vote. From this information they predicted how all the people would vote. This is called a political poll. The pollsters decided that Landon would win the election. James Farley, national chairman of the Democratic party, predicted that Landon would lose the election. In fact, he said that Landon would take only two states, Maine and Vermont. Almost no one believed him.

On election night, in November 1936, Landon went to bed early. He did not need to stay up late to see who would be President. Landon was given the greatest defeat of any candidate in the history of the United States. He received only 8 electoral votes to Roosevelt's 523. He also lost by 11 million popular votes. The pollsters had been wrong. They had not asked the right people. But Jim Farley had been right; Landon won in only two states, Maine and Vermont. There is an old political saying, "As Maine goes, so goes the nation." Farley changed it to "As Maine goes, so goes Vermont."

Alfred Landon in 1969. In his later years he was a special lecturer at Kansas State University.

Landon was surprised by his smashing defeat. He continued to take part in Kansas politics, but eventually retired to private life. His simple ways satisfied Kansas, but they were not enough for a nation in the middle of the Great Depression.

## Thomas E. Dewey
(1902-1971)

George Martin Dewey was one of the founders of the Republican party in the 1850s. Thomas Dewey, his grandson, led that party twice in the race for the White House. Clay and Bryan had run and lost three times, but Dewey was the first two-time presidential loser. Even though he never became President, Dewey is still remembered because of his fine record of fighting against crime in New York.

Dewey was a strong-willed person. He was always well organized, and when he gave orders he expected them to be obeyed. These qualities made him an excellent crimefighter. But Dewey's personality made him seem stiff and formal in public. People had a hard time feeling close to him. The same qualities that made him a good crimefighter made him a poor politician.

Dewey was a short man with a small mustache. He always tried to make himself look taller than he was. When photographers took a picture of him seated at his desk, he sat on a thick telephone book. He even had the ceiling in his office lowered to make him seem taller. His size, his mustache, and his formal personality led people to call him "the little man on the wedding cake."

Harold Stassen, former governor of Minnesota, shakes hands with Thomas E. Dewey before their radio debate. Stassen and Dewey both sought the Republican nomination in 1948.

Dewey began his crimefighting career in 1935. He hired the best men to help him. They set up offices on the 14th floor of the Woolworth Building in New York City. Dewey and his men were hard working, clever, and extremely careful. They tapped phones, checked bank deposits and tax records, and got witnesses to testify. They waited until they had an unbeatable case before arresting anyone. Dewey had a nearly perfect record of successful cases. In a two-year period, he won 71 out of 73 cases. Some of the nation's biggest criminals were put in prison because of Dewey's efforts.

One of the crime rings Dewey broke was the protection racket. Criminals were making businessmen and shop owners pay them for "protection." Men who refused to pay found their businesses damaged. If the owners complained, they were beaten or killed. Dewey brought these racketeers to trial, something no one else had been able to do. By this time he was only 35 years old. He seemed so young that the newspapers called him the Boy Scout.

Dewey and his crimefighting staff are interviewed by reporters in his Woolworth Building headquarters.

Dewey became more and more well known to the American people. In 1937 he was elected district attorney of New York County. He ran for governor of New York in 1938, but he was defeated in a close election. He returned to his position as district attorney and once again began to put lawbreakers in prison. He jailed a group of criminals known as Murder, Incorporated.

Dewey ran for governor of New York again in 1942. This time he was elected. Because he was strong-willed, he was able to get some good laws passed for New York. But many people thought that Dewey was too bossy, that he had too much control of the state legislature. His iron will, as well as his cool manner, kept him from being a popular governor.

By 1944, Dewey thought that it was time for him to run for the presidency. He was nominated by the Republicans to try to beat popular President Roosevelt. This was quite a job for a young man of 42. Not since 1856, when John C. Fremont ran for President, had the Republicans nominated such a young man. When a man announces that he would like to run for President, people sometimes say, "He threw his hat into the ring." One of President Roosevelt's Cabinet members said, "Dewey threw his diaper into the ring."

At the time of the election, the United States was fighting World War II. Unfortunately for Dewey, Americans seemed more interested in finishing the war than in changing Presidents. Dewey was in a difficult position. It would seem disloyal to attack the President. So he said that the nation needed new leaders, not "tired old men." Dewey was a sharp, crisp campaigner. But he had no real issue on which to win support. The people decided to stick with Roosevelt, and he was elected for a fourth term.

Dewey is greeted by some of his New York supporters in 1948.

In 1946 Dewey was re-elected governor of New York, and he remained in the national spotlight. Again, in 1948, he received the Republican nomination for President. This time Harry S Truman was the Democratic candidate. Truman had been Roosevelt's Vice President and had become President in 1945 when Roosevelt died.

Practically everyone expected Dewey to be an easy winner against Truman. Dewey was confident of victory. He ran a well-organized but unexciting campaign. He asked the voters if they had "had enough" of Democratic government, but he was afraid to say anything that might offend anyone. It seemed as if he were just waiting out the time until the election.

Truman was having trouble. He was almost the only person who thought he had a chance to win the election. "Give-'em-hell Harry" started to fight. He went on a long "whistle-stop" tour of the country. He gave short speeches from the back of a train as it stopped at the small communities on the way. He traveled nearly 32,000 miles and made 356 speeches. Many people decided that they liked Truman; he seemed like "one of the folks." Dewey, on the other hand, was a "city slicker." Dewey was forced to try harder. It began to look like a closer election than the Republicans had expected.

Harry Truman speaks from the back
of a train at a small town in Indiana.
Truman's "whistle-stop" campaign
helped him give a surprise defeat to
Thomas Dewey.

When the polls closed on election day, almost everyone thought that Dewey had won. The early voting results showed him ahead. The newspapers were already declaring Dewey the winner. The Chicago *Tribune* headline read: DEWEY DEFEATS TRUMAN. People went to bed believing that Dewey was their next President. But when they awoke, things had changed. The late results from the western states showed that President Truman was the winner by a narrow margin.

Dewey had stayed up all night, and at 5 o'clock in the morning he said that he was "still confident." But at noon that day he had to admit that Truman had won. Thomas Dewey became a two-time loser in one of the great upsets in presidential history.

In 1950 Dewey was elected governor of New York for a third time. When he finished that term in 1954, he retired to private life and once again became a New York lawyer. Then, in 1971, the former district attorney and two-time presidential loser died.

Truman holds an early edition of the Chicago *Tribune*.

Adlai E. Stevenson

# Adlai Stevenson

(1900-1965)

The 1944 and 1948 elections gave the Republican party its first two-time presidential loser. The next two elections gave the Democratic party its first two-time loser, Adlai Stevenson. He was an unsuccessful candidate in 1952 and 1956. Probably the biggest reason for Stevenson's losing those elections was the great popularity of the Republican candidate, Dwight D. Eisenhower. Ike, as General Eisenhower was called, was one of the best liked men in United States history.

Stevenson had many qualities that gained him wide popularity. He was an excellent public speaker. His speeches were pleasant, clever, and witty. Stevenson was well educated; he graduated from Princeton University and then received a law degree from Northwestern University.

A drawing entitled "The Lost Bet." The man who is pulling the carriage had bet that Grover Cleveland and Adlai E. Stevenson (grandfather of Adlai Stevenson) would not win the election of 1892. The man lost his bet.

Stevenson's name was famous. His grandfather, Adlai E. Stevenson, had been Vice President under Grover Cleveland from 1893 to 1897. (He had also run as vice presidential candidate with William Jennings Bryan in 1900.) All these things made Stevenson seem to be a man with a big future.

In 1952 President Truman decided not to run for re-election. His popularity was low with the American people because they suspected that some of the men in his Administration were dishonest. The Democrats began looking for a new candidate. Truman's choice was Stevenson, who was governor of Illinois at that time. But Stevenson said that he was not interested in the presidency. Before the convention some party members, especially in Illinois, began to organize a Draft Stevenson movement. This meant that they would try to get Stevenson nominated even though he had said that he did not want to run. They thought that if Stevenson were chosen by the convention anyway, he could not turn down the nomination.

Luckily for Stevenson's supporters, the Democratic convention was held in Chicago. As governor of Illinois, Stevenson had to give the welcoming speech to the delegates. The party members were impressed with his intelligent and pleasant manner. They gave him a completely unplanned demonstration, clapping and shouting their approval. The Draft Stevenson movement grew, and other candidates began to lose strength. On the third ballot, Stevenson was nominated. Only a very few times in American history has the nomination been given to a man who really did not want to be President.

The Republicans knew that they had a good chance to win in 1952 if they could get a well-known candidate. Their party had been out of the White House for 20 years, and many voters believed that the Democrats had been in power too long. The Republicans asked General Eisenhower to run and he accepted. Both the Democrats and the Republicans had asked Eisenhower to run as their candidate in 1948, but at that time he had turned them down. General Eisenhower had been the leader of the victorious Allied Armies in Europe during World War II.

At their convention in 1952 the Republicans nominated General Dwight D. Eisenhower for President and Senator Richard Nixon for Vice President.

Stevenson and Eisenhower staged an exciting campaign. Ike's gentle, fatherly ways appealed to the public. He had a warm, sincere personality and a friendly grin. The voters seemed to want someone who was more than just a politician. I LIKE IKE buttons were seen almost everywhere.

Stevenson was very popular with certain groups in the country, especially labor union members and college graduates. His intelligence and his clever stories made him a good candidate. Unfortunately, Stevenson was attacked by some people as being too smart. The word "egghead" was first used in this campaign. The term was not directed at Stevenson's high round forehead, but at his intelligence. It was used by people who believed that it was not good for a President to be too smart or too well educated. MADLY FOR ADLAI buttons were not in great demand.

When the election was held, Eisenhower defeated Stevenson easily. He won by such a large margin in the Electoral College (442 to 89 votes) that it was called a "landslide" victory.

The campaign of 1952 was long and difficult. As Stevenson was getting ready to give another speech on his Michigan tour, a photographer took this famous picture of the hole in Stevenson's shoe.

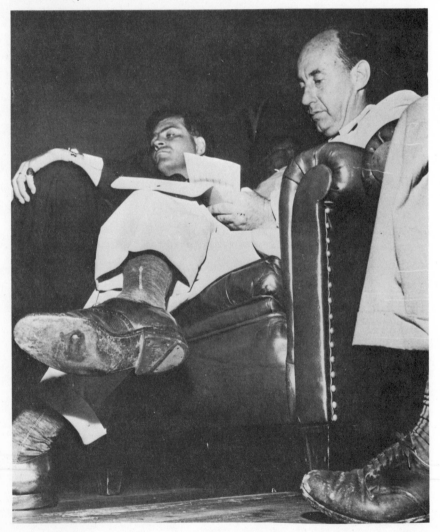

Adlai Stevenson and Estes Kefauver at
the 1956 Democratic national convention

A defeated presidential candidate usually keeps great power within his party. This was true of Stevenson after 1952. He got the Democratic party's presidential nomination again in 1956, even though many of the delegates favored Senator Estes Kefauver of Tennessee. After Stevenson was nominated, the convention chose Kefauver to run for Vice President.

Stevenson shakes hands with John F. Kennedy and Lyndon B. Johnson before the 1960 Democratic convention. The convention nominated Kennedy for President and Johnson for Vice President.

Stevenson's campaign in 1956 was not as lively as it had been in 1952. President Eisenhower had had a heart attack, but he remained just as popular with the American people. The citizens trusted him, and he promised them more peace and prosperity. They felt that the country was in good hands with General Eisenhower in command. Stevenson was defeated again. This time he got only 73 electoral votes to Ike's 457.

The second defeat was enough for Stevenson. He returned to his law practice. His name was voted on at the Democratic convention in 1960, but not enough delegates wanted to give him the nomination for a third time.

Stevenson in the General Assembly hall of the United Nations. President Kennedy appointed him the Permanent Representative of the United States to the United Nations.

In 1961 the new President, John F. Kennedy, called Stevenson back to public service. He appointed Stevenson United States Ambassador to the United Nations. Here was a place in which Stevenson's many talents could be properly used. He became one of the world's most respected statesmen.

Stevenson died in 1965 when he was on an official trip to London. His heart failed while he was walking in the street only a few feet from the American Embassy. Stevenson's death saddened people around the world. They had come to respect the gentle and wise ways of this two-time presidential loser.

Adlai Stevenson walks with Mrs. Eleanor Roosevelt to one of the
1961 sessions of the General Assembly of the United Nations.

## Some Facts About the Electoral College

The electoral college system was set up by the Constitution of the United States. Each state has a group of
electors. The number of electors a state has is equal to the
number of Senators and Representatives that the state has
in the United States Congress. Every state has two Senators
and at least one Representative. States with large populations have more Representatives than states with small
populations. For example, New York has 41 Representatives;
Nevada has 1. New York gets 43 votes in the Electoral
College, but Nevada gets only 3.

Each political party in a state selects its own group of electors. In New York, the Democrats, the Republicans, and all other registered parties choose 43 electors. In Nevada, each party chooses 3 electors. When voters cast their ballots on election day, they are really selecting a group of electors.

Usually the candidate who gets over half the votes in a state gets all of its electoral votes. The members of the Electoral College send their votes to Washington, D. C. About two months after a presidential election, in early January, the electoral votes are counted by the President of the United States Senate.

If no candidate gets a majority in the Electoral College, the House of Representatives is given the job of choosing the President. The House meets in January. The Representatives from each state meet together to decide which candidate to vote for. Each state gets only one vote. The House has had to decide the results of a presidential election three times.

## the author

David J. Goldman is an assistant city attorney for the city of St. Paul, Minnesota. He was formerly on the legal staff of the Federal Communications Commission in Washington, D.C. He received both his bachelor's and law degrees from the University of Minnesota and has also done postgraduate work in American history. Mr. Goldman and his wife Renée live in Minneapolis.

## The Pull Ahead Books

AMERICA'S FIRST LADIES
  1789 to 1865
AMERICA'S FIRST LADIES
  1865 to the Present Day
DARING SEA CAPTAINS
DOERS AND DREAMERS
FAMOUS CHESS PLAYERS
FAMOUS CRIMEFIGHTERS
FAMOUS SPIES
GREAT AMERICAN NATURALISTS
INDIAN CHIEFS
PIRATES AND BUCCANEERS
POLITICAL CARTOONISTS
PRESIDENTIAL LOSERS
SINGERS OF THE BLUES
STARS OF THE ZIEGFELD FOLLIES
WESTERN LAWMEN
WESTERN OUTLAWS

We specialize in publishing quality books for young people. For a complete list please write

*LERNER PUBLICATIONS COMPANY*

*241 First Avenue North, Minneapolis, Minnesota 55401*

M.L. STEELE LIBRARY

T 1470

329
GOL

Goldman, David J. 744138

Presidential losers

| DATE | | |
|---|---|---|
| | | |
| | | |
| | | |
| | | |
| | | |
| | | |
| | | |
| | | |
| | | |
| | | |

Steele High School Library
Amherst, Ohio 44001

© THE BAKER & TAYLOR CO.